MW01538316

Dragonfly

Amazing Fun Facts and Pictures about Dragonfly for Kids

Gaia Carlo

I am a dragonfly.

I am a type of insect.

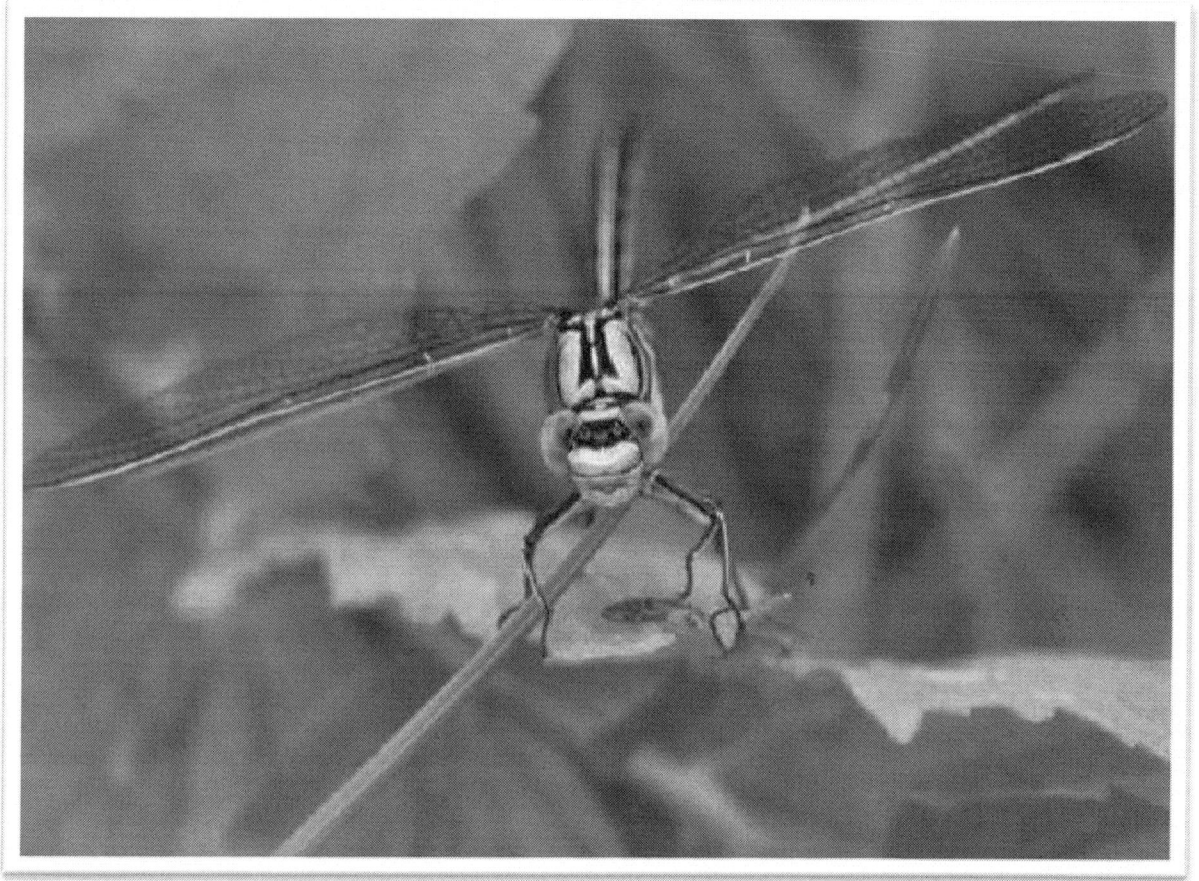

I have two eyes that are very big and can see clearly.

You can find me almost everywhere in the world.

As long as there is water nearby, you can be sure that there will be dragonflies.

I like to live around swamps, streams, lakes and ponds.

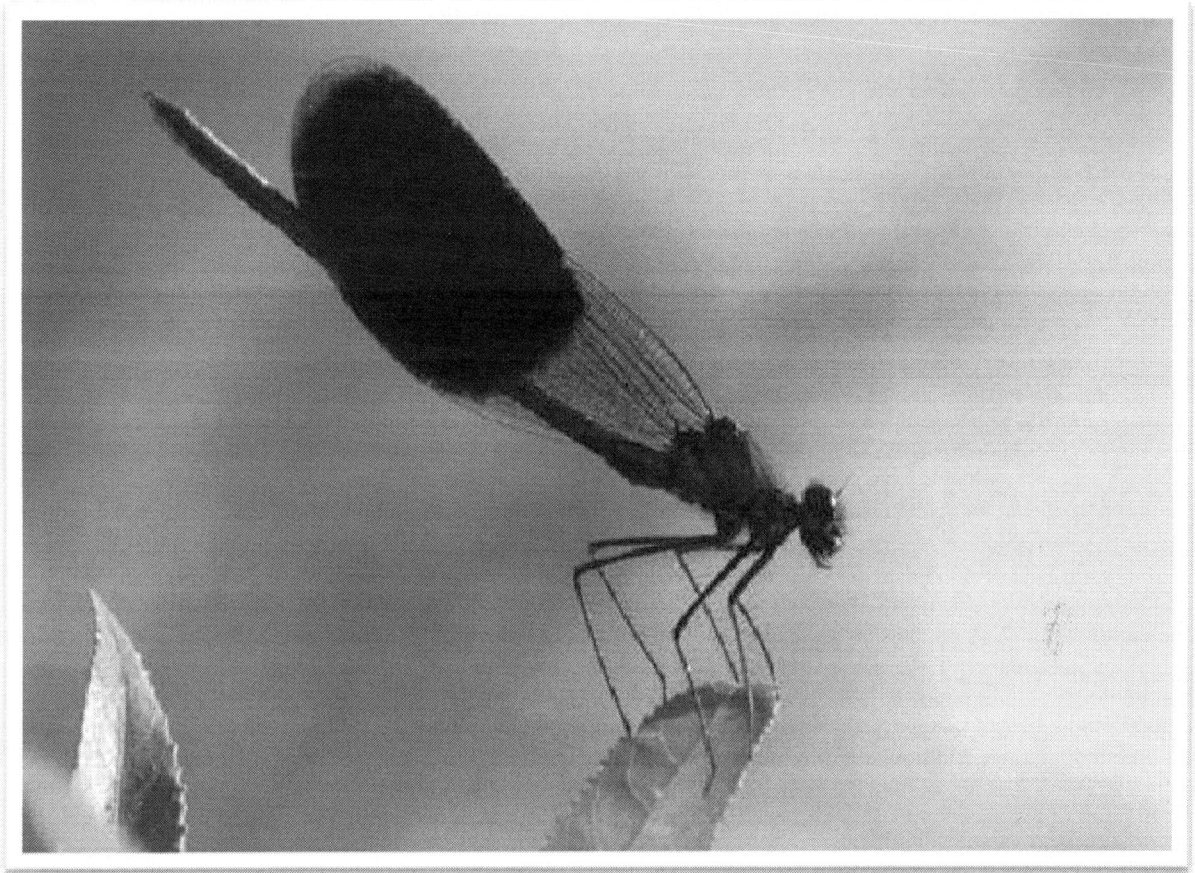

I have four beautiful wings.

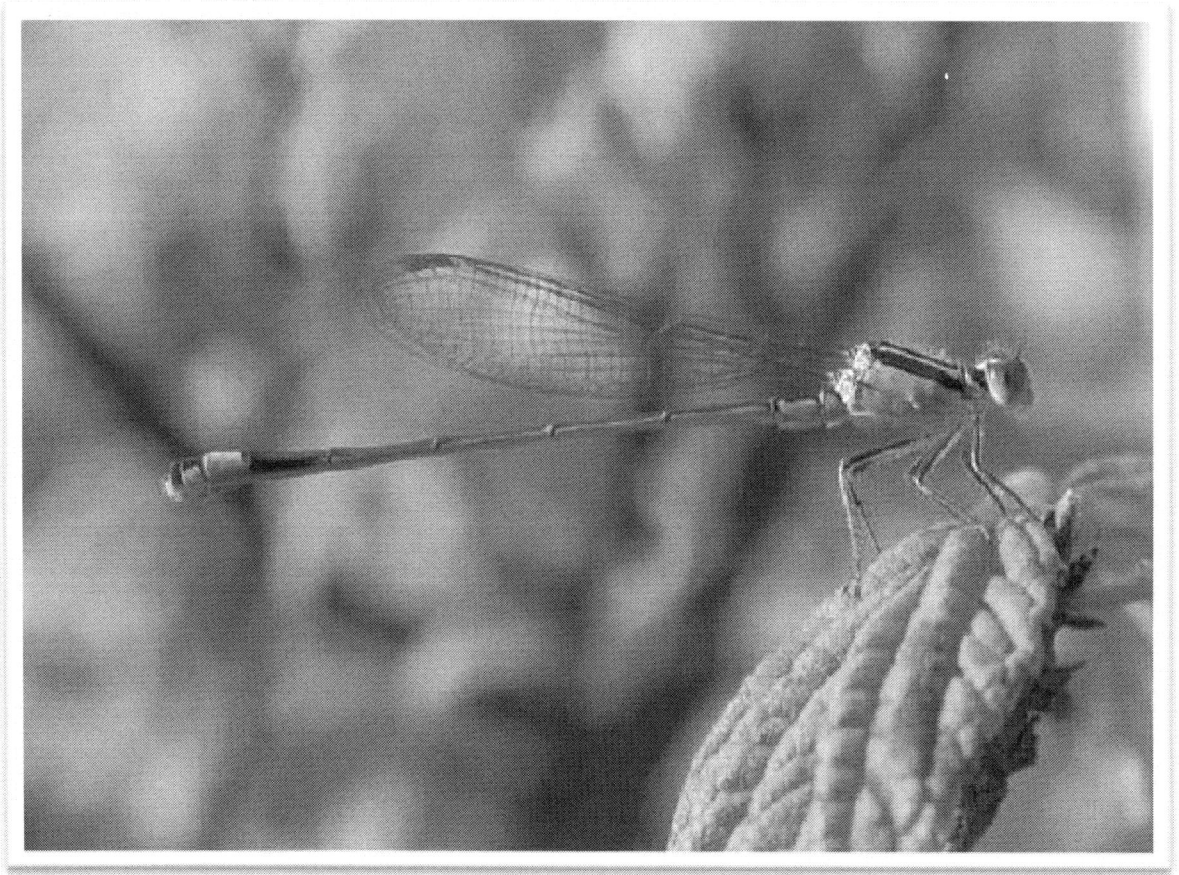

My wings are thin but very colorful.

My wings sparkle in the sunlight.

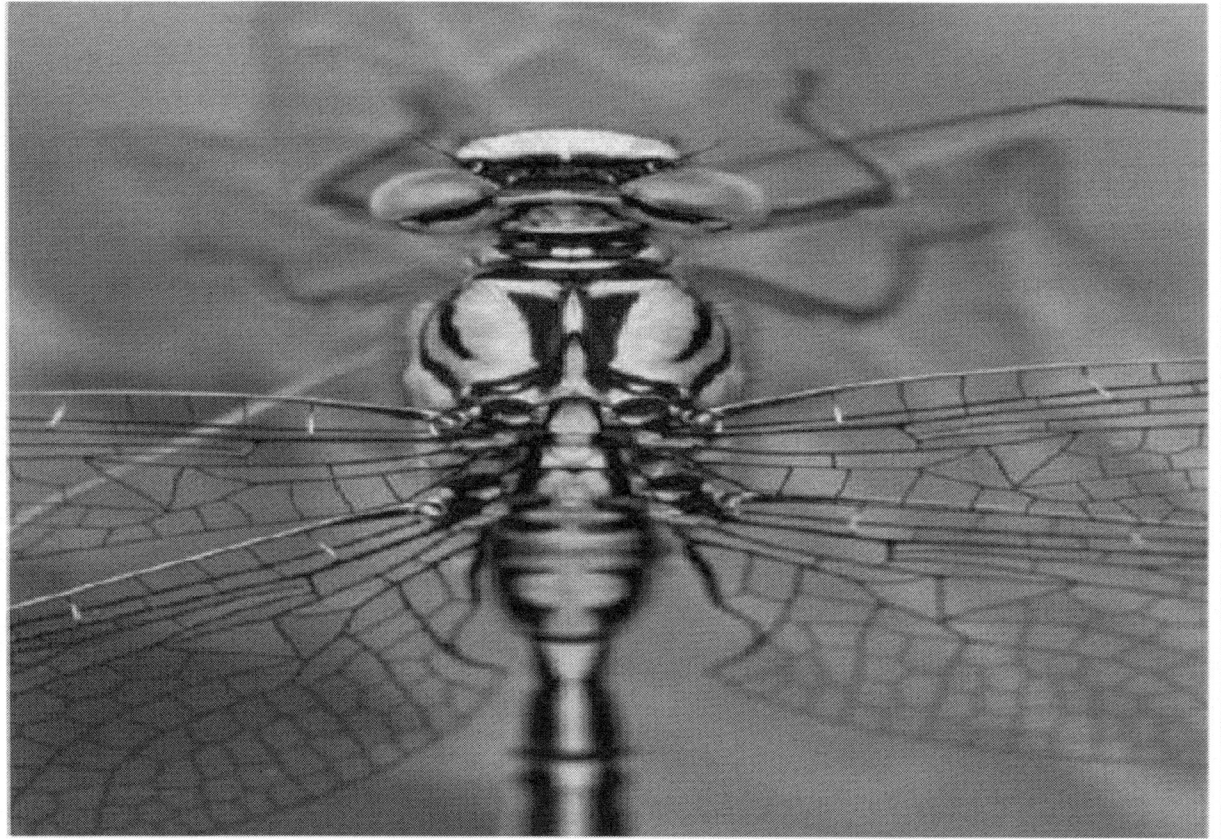

Dragonflies like me come in different colors.

I am one of the best fliers in the world.

I can fly straight up and down and side to side.

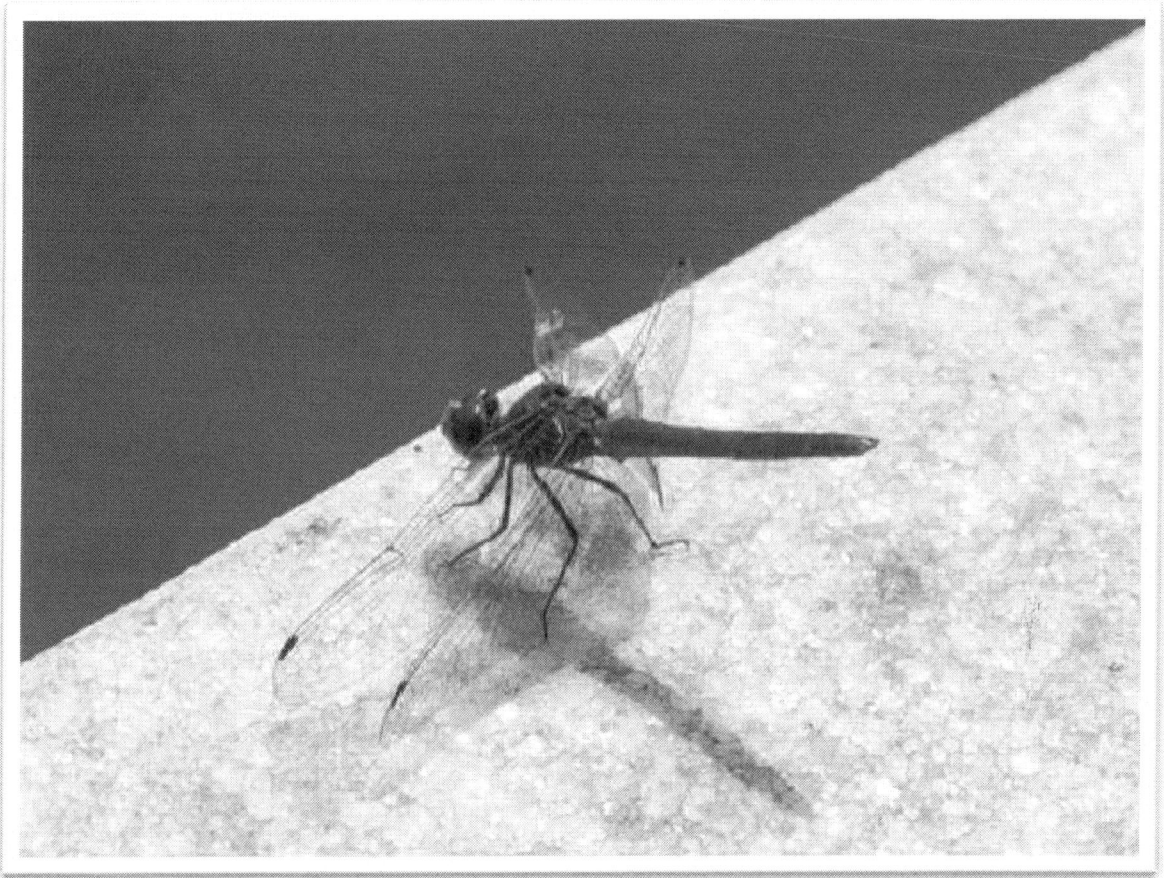

I even catch my food while I am flying.

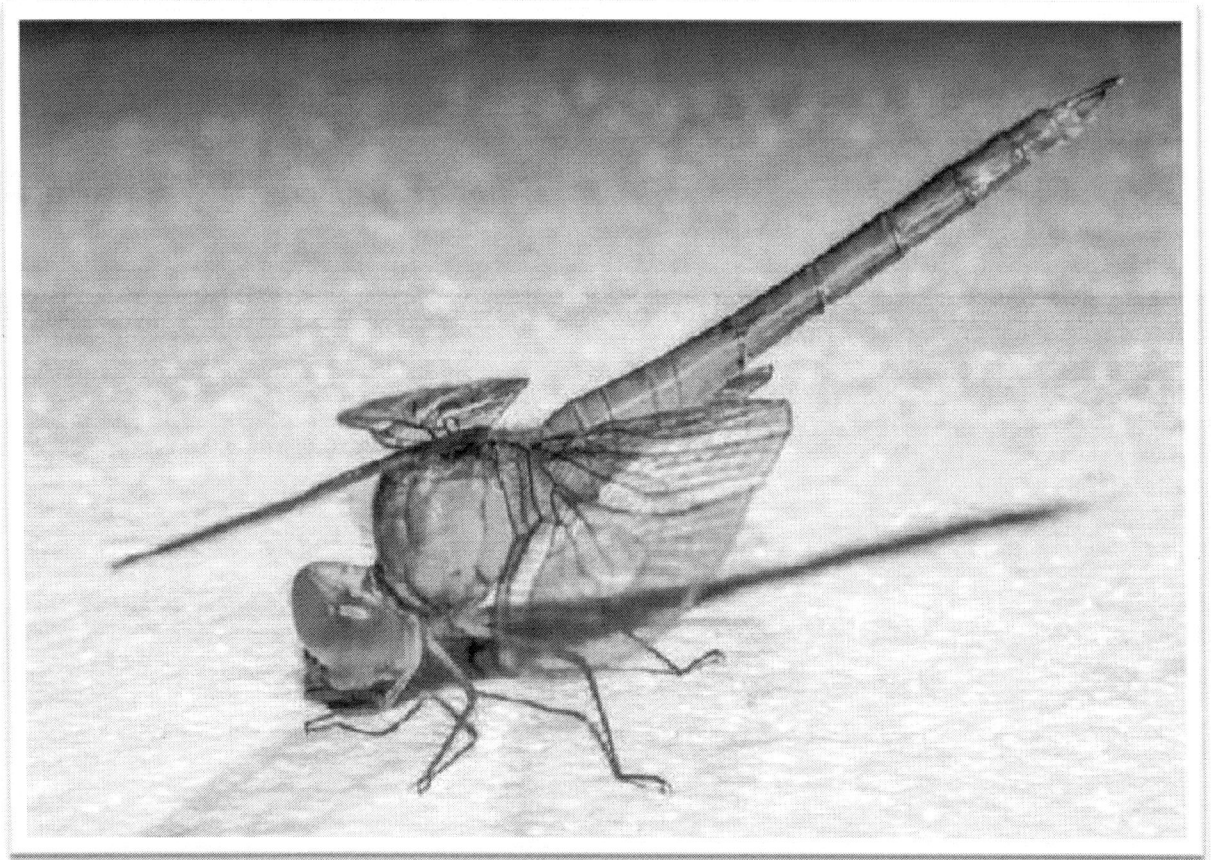

I eat small insects and sometimes I also eat tadpoles and small fish.

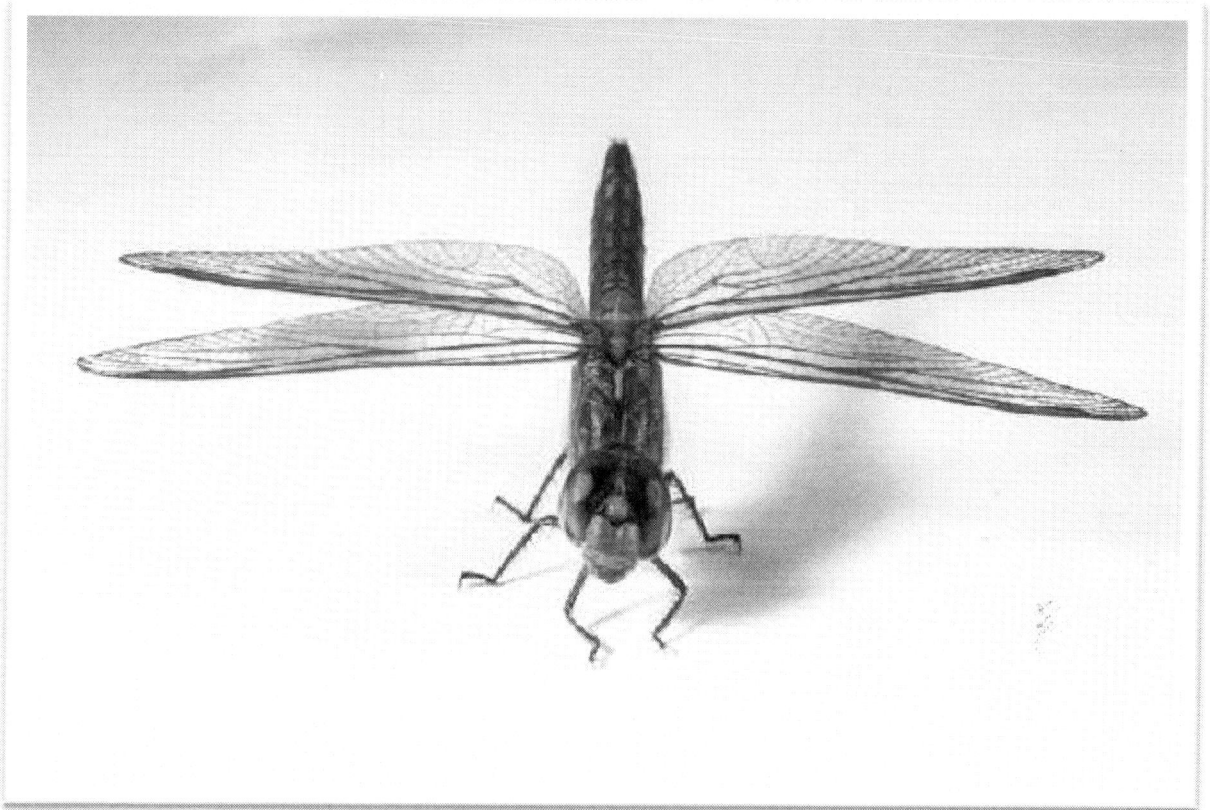

I like to eat small flies, bugs and mosquitoes.

I have six short legs but I cannot walk that good on land.

I use my legs to hold on to my prey.

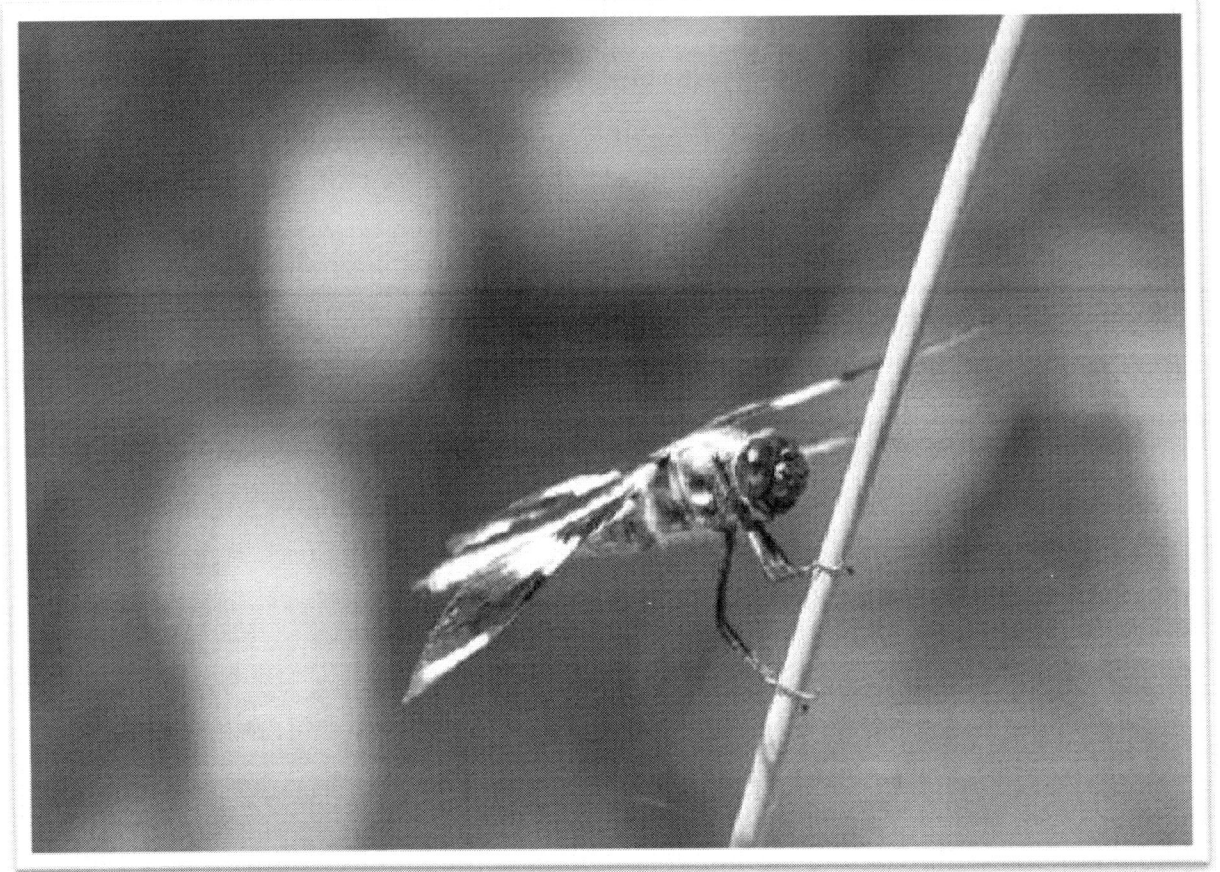

I am afraid of big birds and frogs.

The mama dragonflies lay their eggs on top of the water.

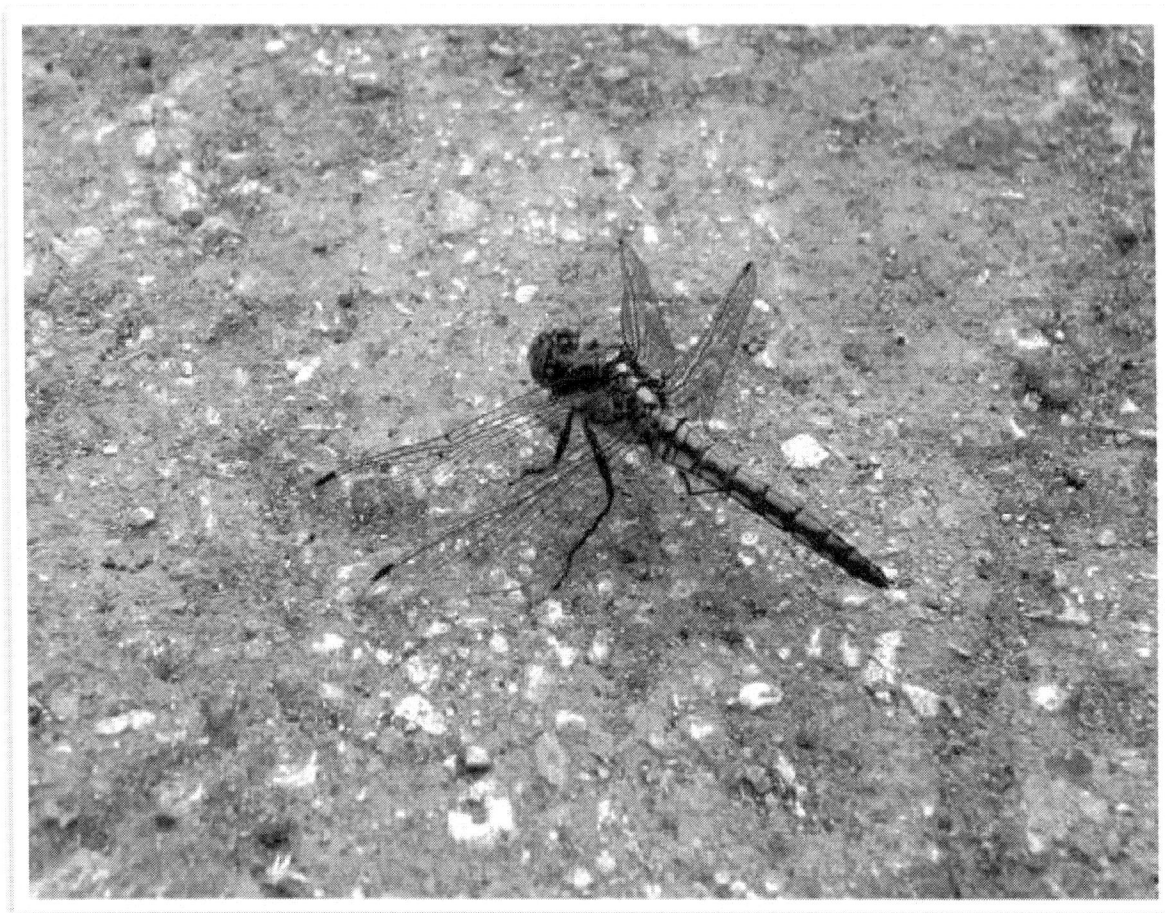

I can live up to a few weeks only.

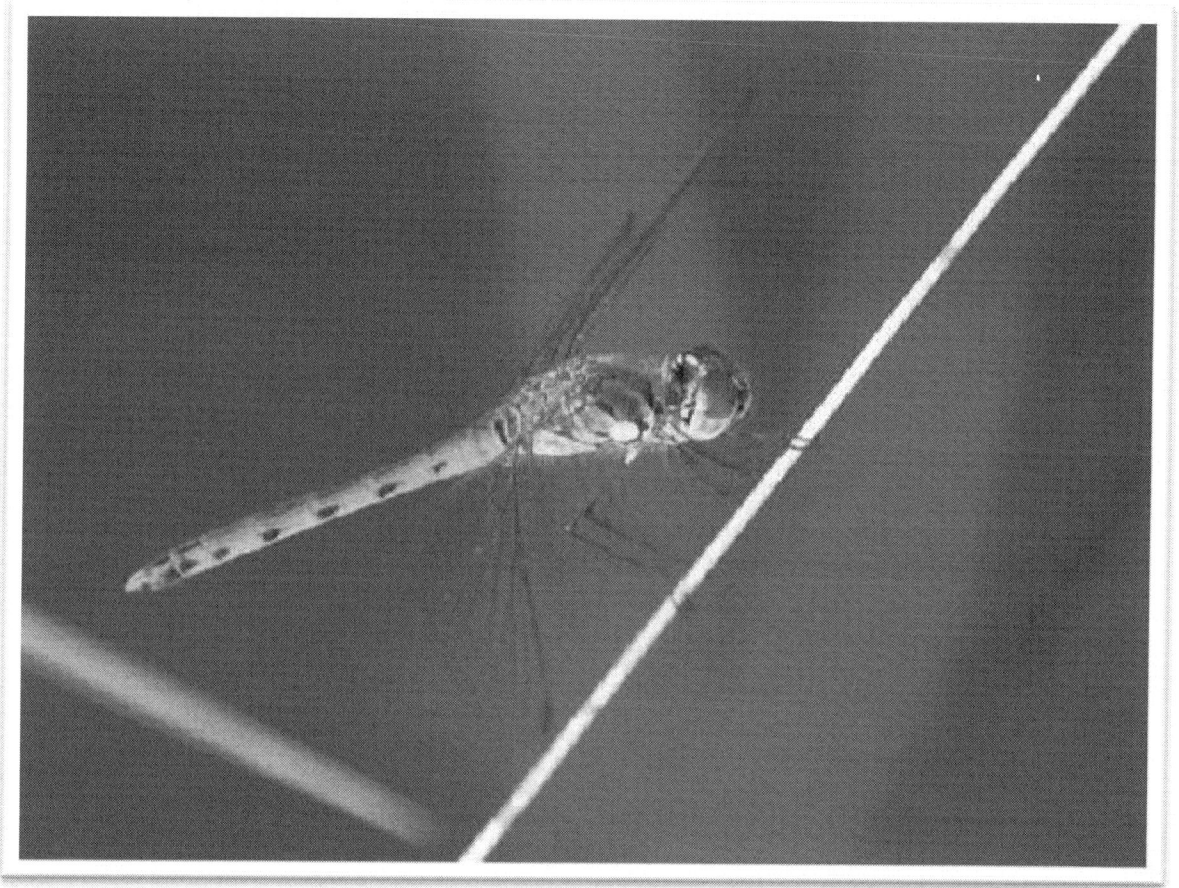

I use my wings to keep me warm when the weather is cold.

I do not sting or bite.

Made in the USA
San Bernardino, CA
02 May 2018